Usborne Beginners
Firefighters

Katie Daynes

Designed by Katrina Fearn and Josephine Thompson

Illustrated by Christyan Fox

KT-524-608

Fire Brigade technical advisor: Andy Pickard
Reading consultant: Alison Kelly, University of Surrey Roehampton

Contents

3 Being a firefighter

4 Fire school

6 Safe clothes

8 At the station

10 Fire engines

12 Tall platforms

14 To the rescue

16 Fighting fires

18 Forest fires

20 Sea and air

22 Accidents

24 Natural disasters

26 Odd jobs

28 Now and then

30 Fire glossary

31 Websites to visit

32 Index

Being a firefighter

Firefighters fight fires and rescue people.
They help in other emergencies too.

Firefighters risk their own
lives to save others.

These firefighters
are tackling a
huge fire.

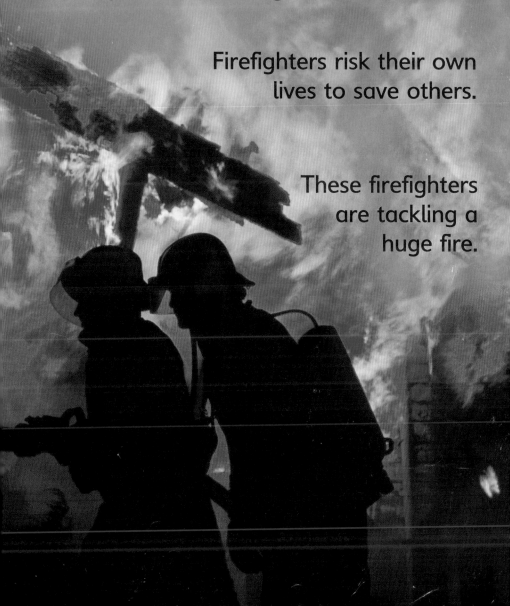

Fire school

Firefighters go to fire school to learn how to do their job. Then they join a fire station and learn more skills.

At fire school, firefighters are taught how to use ladders.

They learn how to put out fires with foam or water.

They also learn how to treat people with injuries.

At fire stations, firefighters play sports once a day to keep fit.

Most fire station yards have a training tower.

Firefighters train by using their ladders and hoses to reach different floors of the tower.

5

Safe clothes

Fires burn through most things, so firefighters wear special outfits to protect themselves.

They wear thick trousers and big heavy boots.

Thick jackets stop the flames from burning the firefighter.

Smoke hood

They have a smoke hood and a helmet to protect their head.

Then they put on thick gloves so their hands don't burn.

When there's lots of smoke, firefighters put on breathing masks.

Bright stripes on their suits help them see each other in the dark.

The boots have metal soles to protect the firefighters' feet.

Firefighters leave their boots inside their trousers so they can put them on quickly.

At the station

All day and all night, firefighters have to be ready to answer an emergency call.

A team arrives for work and reports to the leader.

The firefighters check the fire engines, hoses and tools.

Their meals are cooked in the fire station kitchen.

Firefighters on night duty sleep in beds at the fire station.

In an emergency, an alarm rings and the lights come on.

The firefighters get dressed and rush to their engines.

The engines speed off with their lights flashing and sirens wailing.

Fire engines

Most fire engines carry water and ladders.

Hoses are kept rolled up in here. ——

Water is stored in a big tank inside the engine.

In emergencies, firefighters are allowed to drive faster than the speed limit.

The engine's siren and flashing lights tell drivers it's coming.

They pull over to let the engine speed past them.

This fire engine has a long and a short ladder on its roof.

The driver and five other firefighters travel in the front.

Bright stripes help the engine stand out in busy traffic.

Tall platforms

A platform engine is a fire engine with a platform at the end of a long metal arm.

The engine has four legs that come down to keep it steady.

The driver uses a lever to raise the platform.

The metal arm stretches up and lifts a firefighter above the fire.

This firefighter is squirting water onto a burning building below.

He is wearing a breathing mask so he doesn't breathe in too much smoke.

Some platforms can reach to the top floor of a skyscraper.

To the rescue

If there are people in a burning building, the firefighters' first job is to rescue them.

Firefighters put on breathing masks and check their air tanks.

They write down their names to say they're going into the fire.

Then they enter the building, trailing a line behind them.

Burning buildings are often very smoky.

Heat camera

Firefighters use heat cameras to find trapped people.

The camera senses body heat and shows where people are.

The firefighters then follow their line to find the way out.

Fighting fires

If no one needs rescuing, firefighters try to put out the fire as safely as possible.

They fight big blazes from outside the buildings.

Two engines are sent to most fires, but for huge fires extra engines are called in.

At a small fire, firefighters attach a hose to the fire engine and use water from its tank.

At a big fire, they find a fire hydrant and use water from pipes under the ground.

In the dark, firefighters put up masts with lights so they can see what they're doing.

Forest fires

Fires in forests are hard to put out because trees burn easily.

Careless people often start forest fires.

If it's dry and windy, fires spread quickly.

This fire has spread out of control. The firefighters will call for planes or helicopters to help.

Helicopters carry huge buckets of water to forest fires.

They hover over the fire and drop water onto the flames.

Water bomber planes scoop water from big lakes or the sea and drop it on forest fires.

Sea and air

Fires can happen anywhere. They can be under the ground, in the air and even at sea.

These fire boats are squirting sea water at a fire on an oil tanker.

There was once a fire on a space station. An astronaut put it out with foam.

A light warns a pilot his plane is on fire. He calls the airport and prepares to land.

Some firefighters help the passengers slide to safety while others tackle the fire.

Airports have their own fire engines. They can squirt foam at a fire from a long way away.

Accidents

Firefighters help after road accidents. They have powerful tools that cut through metal.

A car has hit a tree and the driver is trapped.

Firefighters arrive with their cutting tools.

They cut off the roof and help the driver out.

A truck carrying fuel has crashed and toppled over.

Firefighters spray foam on the fuel so it doesn't catch fire.

These firefighters are learning how to break into a car to rescue people.

Natural disasters

After earthquakes or storms, firefighters can be very useful.

An earthquake has made these houses tumble to the ground. Firefighters keep the rubble wet so that fires don't break out.

In a thunderstorm, lightning can start a fire, but the rain often puts it out.

These firefighters have been sent out to help people in a flooded town.

Floods can happen very quickly, leaving people stranded.

Firefighters come to the rescue with life jackets and a boat.

25

Odd jobs

Firefighters do many different jobs. Lots of their jobs have nothing to do with fires.

Firefighters rescue people trapped in lifts or elevators.

They even rescue people who are trapped in railings.

Some firefighters are trained to help people stuck on ice.

This firefighter
is rescuing an
injured man.

He is lowering the man
down a wire to safety.

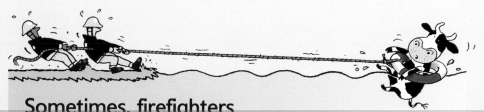

Sometimes, firefighters
are called in to rescue animals.

Now and then

Firefighting has changed a lot over the years, but fire is still just as dangerous.

The first team of firefighters was set up in Rome, a thousand years ago.

Hundreds of years ago, people fought fires by passing buckets of water down a line.

The first fire engines were carts carrying water pumps. They were pulled by horses.

Firefighters used to keep Dalmatian dogs to guard their horses. Now they keep them for good luck.

Modern fire engines are designed to help firefighters tackle fires as quickly as they can.

Fire glossary

Here are some of the words in this book you might not know. This page tells you what they mean.

 emergency – a dangerous situation where extra help is needed.

 training tower – a tall building where firefighters do training exercises.

 breathing mask – a mask that lets firefighters breathe air instead of smoke.

 siren – a device that makes a loud wailing sound. Fire engines have sirens.

 air tank – a container of air, connected to a firefighter's breathing mask.

 heat camera – a camera that senses heat and shows it as a picture.

 fire hydrant – a special pipe firefighters use to get water from underground.

Websites to visit

If you have a computer, you can find out more about firefighters on the Internet. On the Usborne Quicklinks Website there are links to four fun websites.

Website 1 – Visit an online gallery of firefighting vehicles.

Website 2 – Watch a firefighting slide show.

Website 3 – Learn what to do if your clothes catch fire.

Website 4 – Play lots of firefighting games.

To visit these websites, go to
www.usborne-quicklinks.com
and type the keywords "beginners firefighters". Then, click on the link for the website you want to visit. Before you use the Internet, look at the safety guidelines inside the back cover of this book and ask an adult to read them with you.

Index

air tank 14, 30

boat 20, 25

breathing mask 7, 13, 14, 30

clothes 6-7, 31

earthquake 24

fire engines 8, 9, 10-11, 12, 16, 17, 21, 28, 29, 30, 31

fire hydrants 17, 30

fire stations 4, 5, 8-9

floods 25

foam 4, 20, 21, 23

forest fires 18-19

heat camera 15, 30

helicopters 18, 19

hoses 5, 8, 10, 17

ladders 4, 5, 10, 11

lights 9, 11, 17, 21

planes 18, 19, 21

rescue 3, 14-15, 16, 23, 25, 26, 27, 30

siren 9, 11, 30

smoke 7, 13, 15, 30

tools 8, 22

training tower 5, 30

water 4, 10, 13, 17, 19, 20, 28, 30

Acknowledgements

Photographic manipulation by John Russell

Photo credits

The publishers are grateful to the following for permission to reproduce material:
© **Alvey & Towers** 10-11, © **Corbis** title (James L. Amos), 2-3 (Bill Stormont),
9 (J. Barry O'Rourke), 18 (John M. Roberts), 19 (Yves Forestier/Sygma), 20 (Najlah Feanny/Saba),
21 (George Hall), 24 (Roger Ressmeyer), 25 (Kent News & Picture/Sygma), 31 (Royalty-Free);
© **Getty Images** Cover (Wayne R. Bilenduke), 23 (Donovan Reese); © **Powerstock** 7, 16;
© www.shoutpictures.com 13, 15, 17, 29

Every effort has been made to trace and acknowledge ownership of copyright. If any rights have
been omitted, the publishers offer to rectify this in any subsequent editions following notification.

With thanks to

Rosie Kinchen, Jon Costello at Sheffield City Airport and Ty Robinson at Bethnal Green Fire Station

Internet safety rules

- Ask your parent's or guardian's permission before you connect to the Internet.

- When you are on the Internet, never tell anyone your full name, address or telephone number, and ask an adult before you give your email address.

- If a website asks you to log in or register by typing your name or email address, ask an adult's permission first.

- If you do receive an email from someone you don't know, tell an adult and do not reply to the email.

Notes for parents or guardians

The websites described in this book are regularly reviewed and the links in Usborne Quicklinks are updated. However, the content of a website may change at any time and Usborne Publishing is not responsible, and does not accept liability, for the content or availability of any website other than its own, or for any exposure to harmful, offensive or inaccurate material which may appear on the Web. We recommend that children are supervised while on the Internet, that they do not use Internet Chat Rooms and that you use Internet filtering software to block unsuitable material. Please ensure that your children follow the safety guidelines printed above. For more information, see the "Net Help" area on the Usborne Quicklinks website at **www.usborne-quicklinks.com**